Live Without Stress:

30 Days of Finding Christ's Peace for Your Soul

How to Overcome Anxiety and Stress Through Christ's Transforming Power

Live Without Stress:
30 Days of Finding Christ's Peace for Your Soul

by Shelley Hitz

All rights reserved. No part of this publication may be reproduced, stored in a retrieval system, or transmitted by any means – electronic, mechanical, photographic (photocopying), recording, or otherwise – without prior permission in writing from the author, unless it is for the furtherance of the Gospel of salvation and given away free of charge.

Body and Soul Publishing
ISBN-13: 978-0615670751
ISBN-10: 061567075X

All scripture quotations are taken from the New King James Version®. Copyright© 1982 by Thomas Nelson, Inc. Used by permission. All rights reserved.

Learn more information at:
www.BodyandSoulPublishing.com

Contents

Introduction 1
Day 1: Trusting God 2
Day 2: The Truth 4
Day 3: No Fear 6
Day 4: Be Prepared 8
Day 5: No Worries 10
Day 6: Prayerful Planning 12
Day 7: Be Still 14
Day 8: Prayer Connection 16
Day 9: The Uncontrollable 18
Day 10: Trials 20
Day 11: No Sweat 22
Day 12: Casting Burdens 24
Day 13: Peace-Maker 26
Day 14: Organization 28
Day 15: Out of My Hands 30
Day 16: Unnecessary 32
Day 17: Stress Filter 34
Day 18: Stress Outlet 36
Day 19: Conflict Resolution 38
Day 20: Relaxation 40
Day 21: Moving Forward 42
Day 22: Constructive Communication 45
Day 23: Medicating Stress 47
Day 24: Talk it Out 49
Day 25: Balancing Life 52
Day 26: Achieving Peace 55
Day 27: Praise & Worship 57
Day 28: Stressful Situations 59
Day 29: No Pressure 61
Day 30: Pursuing Christ 63
Conclusion: 65

Introduction

Do you get stressed out by people and circumstances in your life? Most people do, but that isn't how God designed us to live. He doesn't want us to live a life full of stress, anxiety or fear, but a life of trust, hope, and joy. He doesn't want us to worry, but to put our faith in Him and trust Him to provide for all of our needs.

This book is designed for you to read one reading per day, and our hope that over the next 30 days you can overcome the stress and anxiety in your life, being transformed through Christ's amazing power. We know that while in this world we will have trouble, we can take heart in the fact that Jesus has overcome the world. When we put our faith in Him, we have no reason to stress, worry, or fear.

"These things I have spoken to you, that in Me you may have peace. In the world you will have tribulation; but be of good cheer, I have overcome the world."
John 16:33

Day 1: Trusting God

I can handle all stress by trusting God.

Trust in Him at all times, you people; Pour out your heart before Him; God is a refuge for us.
                                                Psalm 62:8

Stress may be a fact of life, but I am equipped to handle it positively by trusting in God, and thus I am strengthened.

It is healthier to manage my stress in a positive manner by trusting God rather than to allow it to affect me negatively. When I make the choice to trust God with what I am stressed about, I am able to quickly deal with the cause of stress. And by coping with the cause of stress effectively, I give myself the opportunity to reduce or eliminate my stress levels permanently.

By allowing God to deal with my stress, my character is strengthened. **I am able to create a positive attitude within myself through trust in God even when faced with worry.**

I feel a sense of confidence because I know God can manage my stress swiftly and positively. This is because God will give me the time, patience, energy, and tools necessary to manage stressful situations without succumbing to the stress.

God has given me the ability to use positive, healthy coping skills to deal with the stress in my life. I am far less likely to become overwhelmed in stressful situations when I know how to handle them in a positive, peaceful manner and remember that God is in complete control.

Today I will choose to fix my mind on "whatever is true, whatever is noble, whatever is right, whatever is pure, whatever is lovely, whatever is admirable-if anything is excellent or praiseworthy" in my life to help me to deal with my stress (Phil 4:8). *I will continue trusting God so I can train myself to focus on what He is accomplishing through me.* By doing this, I help my mind to react positively when stress occurs.

Self-Reflection Questions:

1. What is the greatest source of stress in my life? What will I do about it today?

2. How does trusting in God help me deal with stress?

3. What tools can I use to manage stress positively?

Day 2: The Truth

Stressful moments do not blind me from what is true.

For God so loved the world that He gave His only begotten Son, that whoever believes in Him should not perish but have everlasting life.
John 3:16

I am confident in my beliefs, so stress does not blind me from what I know to be true.

I know, for example, that with God's guidance, **what I view as mistakes are merely stepping stones to greater things.** I have let go of the idea that I have to get everything right the first time I try.

I let go of the paralysis that comes from expecting perfection and, instead, I am content with putting my best foot forward. Even when I think I make mistakes, I know that God is moving me in the right direction.

I am also confident in the love of God. While I don't always know why things happen, He is working out His plan of love in my life. He loves me enough to send His Son to die for me. He will not desert me now.

Because I know this to be true, **I have a solid foundation to rely on in the face of stress.**

I take comfort in the presence of the Father. While I have much left to learn, I know that my Creator is an ever-present reality in my life. I trust that **my Savior will help me create something beautiful and meaningful** from whatever challenges come my way.

Self-reflection Questions:

1. Do I allow myself to trust the permanent nature of God's love for me?

2. Do I believe in the ability to grow from mistakes?

3. Am I allowing God to create something good out of my challenges?

Day 3: No Fear

Fear cannot penetrate my inner being.

There is no fear in love; but perfect love casts out fear, because fear involves torment. But he who fears has not been made perfect in love.
I John 4:18

I enjoy living a life free from fear. I take action every day that helps keep it at bay and if it does try to creep into my mind, the minute I feel the first inklings of it, **I banish it in Jesus' name.** It runs away like the cowardly thing it is, disappearing into the darkness from whence it came!

My unfailing trust in Christ is part of my mindset that helps keep fear away. When scary things happen, I trust the best ending to the situation, and usually I get it. When challenges arise, I trust God to lead me to a solution, and usually I find one.

I meditate on God's Word every day and this helps provide an ongoing shield against fear. In my meditations on scripture, I visualize joy and peace. There is no room for fear here. **I maintain peace and serenity with my thoughts.**

If I should start to feel fear, I replace the negative thoughts with positive images and affirmations from scripture. *I remind myself that Christ in me is stronger than fear* and that fear has no hold over me.

I take action through prayer to do what I can to make every situation better. When my mind is focused on prayer, **there is no time for worrying,** so, once again, I command fear to leave my mind and replace it with something positive.

Today, I plan to enjoy a carefree day without fear, sailing through my day's journey on a calm sea of trust in Christ, joy and peace.

Self-Reflection Questions:

1. What do I fear?

2. What can I take action through prayer to banish my fears and replace them with positive thoughts from God's Word?

3. How much time do I sit around worrying about the *"what ifs,"* instead of taking action through prayer to bring about beneficial results?

Day 4: Be Prepared

A little prayer and preparation takes me a long way in easing strain and stress.

The plans of the diligent lead surely to plenty, but those of everyone who is hasty, surely to poverty.
                                                                    Proverbs 21:5

Being prepared makes living my life easier. I am so glad that I have discovered ways to effectively manage my everyday life.

Choosing to proactively pray and prepare for the day is such a simple way for me to remove stress from my life. Just a little prayer and preparation make such a big difference in my attitudes and perspectives.

Every morning, I take a few moments to spend with God and pray about my commitments for the day. I also jot down a list of things I need to accomplish so I can stay focused on my goals. Knowing my deadlines and prioritizing my tasks is an effective way to ease the strain in my life.

When I have an important deadline approaching, I pray about it and enlist the help of others. I also make schedules and set aside time to work on the project. Making clear plans and remembering God is in control is a great way to ease anxiety. Since I take actions to keep my projects on schedule, I am confident that God will help me reach my goals. ***Preparing and trusting in God for success ensures that I succeed.***

The stress I once had in my life is gone because I have taken proactive steps toward organizing my life, and acknowledging God's provision. Anxiety can be prevented. I am so relieved to have found systems that help me manage my life.

I am ready for any project and each task I approach seems more manageable. *Prayer and preparation are useful tools that I implement in my life.* I am ready to succeed because I am prepared.

Self-Reflection Questions:

1. How do I prepare for the tasks and projects in my life?

2. How do prayer and preparation ease my stress and strain?

3. How could I take a more proactive approach to reach my goals?

Day 5: No Worries

I refuse to worry when priorities change.

For I know the thoughts that I think toward you, says the LORD, thoughts of peace and not of evil, to give you a future and a hope.
Jeremiah 29:11

I let go of unrealistic expectations. It's not possible to see all the way to the end of my life and to anticipate every change along the way, only God can do that.

When my priorities change – as they will, likely again and again over the course of my life – I entrust God with my future. Things may not be part of my original plan, but I trust in Him that everything will work out anyway.

By letting go of worry and trusting in God, I free up my energy to find the best and most constructive way of dealing with the situation at hand.

By accepting the situation and letting go of my ideas of what could have, should have, or might have been, I release myself to discover and draw out all that is inherently good in my new, God given, circumstances. **Only by being open to change and trusting in God can I truly discover all that He has in store for me.**

I let go of the impulse to sit down in the road and sulk because it took a twist I wasn't expecting. I recognize that going backward is an impossibility. So I keep moving forward with the Holy Spirit as my guide, knowing that **walking down an unexpected path is still progress**, no matter if the scenery may have changed.

Self-Reflection Questions:

1. How do I respond when my circumstances change unexpectedly?

2. Do I remain open to change so I can continually learn and grow?

3. How can I make the best of an unexpected situation?

Day 6: Prayerful Planning

Prayerful planning allows me to complete my tasks without stress.

> *In his heart a man plans his course, but the LORD determines his steps.*
> Proverbs 16:9

Having a prayed out plan allows me to stay on track and complete my tasks easily without undue stress. With each step, I feel achievement as part of the plan is completed.

Plans remind me of the action steps I need to take at each point. Always knowing what to do enables me to push extraneous concerns aside and achieve success with the help of Christ.

I complete one step at a time and move on to the next with ease. As I complete one task at a time, I am able to build moment toward the end goal.

When stress threatens, I can rely on God to get me through and I keep moving forward. Since my tasks have already been laid out for me, I simply forge on, confident that my actions will move me closer to my goals.

God helps me transform stress into a motivator that pushes me further and farther than I've ever been. I know that without Him, my plans would be in vain.

Today I will complete my tasks more easily, knowing that ***I am fully capable of great things through Christ.*** By following prayed out plans, I can disregard my worries and focus on completing my tasks with God's help.

Self-Reflection Questions:

1. How does having a plan help me?

2. How does stress keep me from achieving my goals?

3. What is my next action step in my plan?

Day 7: Be Still

Faith in Christ enables me to find peace of mind.

Be still, and know that I am God; I will be exalted among the nations, I will be exalted in the earth! The LORD of hosts is with us; The God of Jacob is our refuge.
Psalm 46:10-11

During the day, I take time to spend with Christ. When I pray I confess my stress to Him, trusting that He is in control.

My worries diminish as I shift my focus to God's sovereignty. The more my faith grows, the more my stress is debilitated. The power of my worries dwindles with each minute that I spend with Christ.

I use breathing techniques to help me calm down. As I breathe in slow, deep breaths, I envision the *Holy Spirit* entering my body. As I breathe out, I see my tension and worries being carried away. With my eyes shut, I spend time just listening to God's voice.

Relaxing is important to me because I know that **if I can trust God with my thoughts, He will comfort and guide me.** I have given God authority over my thoughts. My worries are powerless over me. My faith in Christ melts away my anxieties.

When the pace of life becomes too fast for me to keep up, I remove myself from it in order to refocus. *I have a quiet place* where I go to be still before my God.
Free time is something that I embrace and enjoy. I am comfortable when I spend private time with God. I write God's name in my planner. Having dates with Him helps me stay in touch with who He created me to be.

Soft music helps me relax. My favorite sound is the ocean surf. Each time I hear a crashing wave, I visualize God's power to wash my sins and worry away.

I am proud of myself for making God a priority and treating my relationship with Him with the value and importance that it deserves. As a result, treasures are unlocked deep within me, and I rest my head in the hands of His peace that surpasses all understanding.

Self-Reflection Questions:

1. Is my breathing short and shallow or deep and slow?

2. What tools could I use to help me be still before my Creator?

3. How do I unwind and recharge after a long day?

Day 8: Prayer Connection

Prayer is my rock during stressful moments.

Let your gentleness be evident to all. The Lord is near. Do not be anxious about anything, but in every situation, by prayer and petition, with thanksgiving, present your requests to God. And the peace of God, which transcends all understanding, will guard your hearts and your minds in Christ Jesus.
Philippians 4:5-7

Prayer is my connection to Jesus, the source of peace. When I am stressed, praying helps me to stay calm.

I stand firm on prayer when the waves of uncertainty come my way.

Prayer is my way of getting my inner self into focus. When I feel myself getting overwhelmed by responsibilities, I am able to pray as a way to clear my mind and organize my thoughts.

When I pray, I build up my faith. I speak to my Creator, sharing my fears, thoughts, and feelings. I pray in a quiet place, where I can shut off the noise from the world.

After I pray, I sit in silence and wait. I listen to the voice of peace that speaks to me in stillness.

When I pray, I strengthen the core muscles of my being. Prayer keeps me from drowning in fear and stress.

I strengthen my mind against negativity by meditating on God's Word, the Bible. His Word is stronger than negative thoughts. When I meditate on scripture I think of things that are pure, lovely, and right.

Whatever I set my mind on, I become. Therefore, I think lofty thoughts and set my mind on things above. ***Prayer is an act of faith.*** I know that there is someone bigger than me who cares for me.

I do not have to face the world alone. What a joy it is to know that I do not have to figure everything out by myself! There are ears ready to hear me when I call. All I have to do is sit quietly in prayer and Jesus is there with me.

Self-Reflection Questions:

1. How can I increase the time I spend in prayer and meditation on God's Word?

2. What is an important prayer that I have today?

3. What have I set my mind on?

Day 9: The Uncontrollable

I trust God with the things I cannot control.

No temptation has overtaken you except such as is common to man; but God is faithful, who will not allow you to be tempted beyond what you are able, but with the temptation will also make the way of escape, that you may be able to bear it.

1 Corinthians 10:13

When I am faced with a situation that is out of my control, I remain calm by putting my faith in Christ. I simply place the situation in God's hands and walk away. Patiently, I wait for Him to provide the answers. While I wait, I am relaxed and confident. I let go of the need to control every situation.

My thoughts are focused on the things I can control. God has given me freewill; my thoughts and actions are under my command. By exercising self-control, I am a source of encouragement in difficult situations.

Things I cannot control roll off my back like water off a swan. I do not dwell on things beyond my control because I accept my limits and put my trust in Christ. I know that God provides a solution to every problem.

Understanding that things don't always go my way, **I humble myself to the sovereignty of God.** What I *can* do is keep a positive attitude even when I don't get my way.

If I feel myself getting frustrated over something beyond my control, I remove myself from the situation and pray. Taking a warm bath lets me soak my cares away. Using praise and worship, I cleanse myself of the desire to control what I cannot.

I accept that I cannot control others. Without using manipulation, I try to help and influence others, but I do not expect them to bend to my will. **Even when I think there is a better way, I am a team player.** I do not value my own point of view above everyone else's opinion. I pray for God's will to be done, not my own.

When I trust in Christ I am free from insecurity. My mind is focused on positive things. I am mature enough to accept the bad with the good, and what I cannot control with what I can. I have peace and hope.

Self-Reflection Questions:

1. What are the things that I can control?

2. How can I keep my peace when things don't go my way?

3. How can I influence others without being controlling?

Day 10: Trials

I wholly accept difficulties in my life. God is using my trials to perfect me.

My brethren, count it all joy when you fall into various trials, knowing that the testing of your faith produces patience. But let patience have its perfect work, that you may be perfect and complete, lacking nothing.
James 1:2-4

I accept that trials are in an inevitable part of my life and I let go of the idea that life in this world will ever be perfect. Instead, I recognize them as a valuable asset in my life, one that God is using to perfect my faith.

I appreciate the way that the trials in my life encourage me to cry out to God. They produce faith and patience within me. When I am stressed I know something in my spiritual life needs to be addressed.

Trials help sharpen my spiritual focus so I can concentrate and have clarity when I pray. They make me more acutely aware of what is going on in my life and push me to seek the Word of God and apply it to my circumstances.

I count my trials as joy, allowing God to use them to complete me. However, **I turn to Christ at the first sign of trouble**, rather than as a last resort. I resist the impulse to ignore my stress allowing it to take a toll on my health and well-being.

By paying attention to my body's signals, I can tell which areas of my spiritual life need work. But there are times when I realize that I let a trial get the best of me. When this happens, I view it as a sign to step back, pray, and seek God's guidance. Then, when I have done so, I can carry on, with the trial in its rightful place as a healthy partner in my life.

Self-Reflection Questions:

1. Do I view trials as an enemies or allies?

2. Do I pay attention and respond when stress signals that something is wrong?

3. Do I allow myself to regroup when trials get the best of me?

Day 11: No Sweat

I do not sweat the small stuff.

"Therefore do not worry, saying, 'What shall we eat?' or 'What shall we drink?' or 'What shall we wear?' For after all these things the Gentiles seek. For your heavenly Father knows that you need all these things. But seek first the kingdom of God and His righteousness, and all these things shall be added to you. Therefore do not worry about tomorrow, for tomorrow will worry about its own things. Sufficient for the day is its own trouble.
Matthew 6:33

Little things that are happening around me cause me no concern.

Through Christ, I maintain a calm feeling in my daily life and with His strength, I can handle the little things that go awry around me. Often when things happen that are out of my control I can look at them and laugh at the irony of the situation.

Life is interesting and things happen every day that are out of my control. This is okay; it adds to the interest. I can remain calm when little incidents happen because they do not hinder my day or my life in any way that I cannot manage in Christ's strength.

Often the little incidents that happen are kind of funny. Today I can find the humor in these situations. *I can remain calm throughout these situations because I have the presence of Christ, a base of calmness, that surrounds me.*

I seek out Jesus who gives me peace and a calm state of mind on a daily basis; this helps me to avoid unnecessary worry over the little things that happen in life. I surround myself in His presence, a blanket of calmness, by spending time with Jesus and in solitude. I also get the rest that I need, avoiding over-scheduling, and allow myself to enjoy my hobbies. *Christ's presence, this blanket of calmness surrounding me, protects me from life's little upsets.*

Today I will make sure I am surrounded by Christ, my protection of calmness and which will enable me to endure life's little quirks and upsets. I will remain calm, regardless of what may come. *I will learn to laugh instead of worry.*

Self-Reflection Questions:

1. Have I covered myself in Christ's presence, a blanket of calmness?

2. Have I sought out the humor in life's little upsets?

3. Have I taken an initiative to remain calm?

Day 12: Casting Burdens

I give my problems to God and have no reason to harbor tension.

Cast your burden on the LORD, and He shall sustain you; He shall never permit the righteous to be moved.
Psalm 55:22

God can handle everything. I am open and unresisting, and I know **tension and negative thoughts do not control me**. They merely are passing through as quickly as they arrived, I can trust God with anything that comes my way.

Whatever I nurture becomes a part of me. It expands, grows, and puts down roots. Because I nurture peace, I am confident that God will increase it within me.

I am unafraid of stressful thoughts and feelings. **Tension has no traction in my life because I let it flow through me and away, trusting in God's provision.** This makes room for more peaceful thoughts. Peace and tension cannot co-exist. Whatever I nurture will thrive.

Because I choose to nurture peace, God creates an inner atmosphere conducive to improved health and creativity within me. I see no purpose in harboring tension. Instead, and let flow away from me, casting all my cares on God my Father.

I take a moment to be alone with God and relax when I feel tension rising within me. I close my eyes, and pray. I focus on God's promises and provision.

I know that **my natural state as a believer in Christ is one of calmness and peace,** and that trusting in God will allow Him to return me to this state. I let go and allow myself to return to the state of peace and harmony that my Creator has instilled within me.

Self-Reflection Questions:

1. Do I nurture peace or tension?

2. How do I respond when I feel tension rising?

3. How can I set up opportunities to relax and pray?

Day 13: Peace-Maker

I will remain calm through prayer and trust in God.

He who has knowledge spares his words, and a man of understanding is of a calm spirit. Even a fool is counted wise when he holds his peace...
Proverbs 17:27-28

It is okay to reject pressure and disarray. When I find myself in uncomfortable situations, I can take a step back in order to remain calm.

I keep my wits about me in the face of conflict. **I am a peace-maker.** My emotions are under control.

Regardless of how heated a situation becomes, I keep a soft tone of voice. When necessary, I stop and pray in order to delay an inappropriate reaction. I take deep breaths to help me stay calm.

I allow myself to feel secure. The tranquility God has given me has healed me from anxiety and I remain calm so that my view will be clear.

When I am calm, I make intelligent choices. If I let my emotions dictate my behavior, I know I will have regrets. Instead, relying on God helps me live a life of integrity.

To keep a sense of calm, I bear a load that is just right for me. *I refuse to overload myself.* Saying *no* to extra responsibilities is something I do in order to protect myself from a nervous breakdown.

My eating habits are healthy. I make sure that I get enough sleep in order to rejuvenate my body and mind. *Living a healthy lifestyle helps me to be calm.* Throughout the day, I take quiet pauses to pray in order to stay fresh and focused.

Worrying is a pointless waste of time. I know that worrying won't add a single hour to my life or provide clothes for me to wear, so I choose to pray about the things I cannot change and plan for those that I can.

Self-Reflection Questions:

1. What are some activities that have a calming effect on me?

2. What are some activities or places that make me tense?

3. How do I benefit from staying calm?

Day 14: Organization

Because I am organized, I am able to minimize my daily stress.

For which of you, intending to build a tower, does not sit down first and count the cost, whether he has enough to finish it-
Luke 14:28

I take the necessary time to be organized because I know that doing so minimizes my daily stress. While it is sometimes tempting to rush into a work week or a project, I recognize that my time is like money; I have to spend some to gain some.

I prayerfully organize my time to facilitate my goals by pruning off activities that drain me of my time and energy, and always seeking God's will for my life. I recognize that, like everyone else, my time is not limitless. I choose to set aside specific times for those activities that are important to me and I let the rest go.

I set aside time at the beginning of each project to **pray and make sure I have a clear picture of where I am going** and that I have the resources I need to get there. This way I don't end up whittling it away on pointless and avoidable activities.

For example, I see no point in wasting time hunting for my keys each morning, so I set a basket by the door to drop them in each night.

Supplies are stocked and organized by my desk to prevent wasted time and distraction when I am in the middle of my work.

A weekly menu eliminates waste when I shop and minimizes my time in the kitchen.

I take a few minutes to prayerfully do each of these things on a periodic basis so I can have more time to focus on what is truly important in my life.

Self-Reflection Questions:

1. What excuses do I give myself for not being organized?

2. What frequent time wasters can be minimized or eliminated?

3. What can I do, today, to begin the process of getting organized?

Day 15: Out of My Hands

I can manage stress because I know I cannot control everything.

> ...my speech and my preaching were not with persuasive words of human wisdom, but in demonstration of the Spirit and of power, that your faith should not be in the wisdom of men but in the power of God.
>
> 1 Corinthians 2:4-5

I can manage stress because I accept my limits and trust God with what is out of my hands. I am only one person and my energy and resources are limited so I let go of the idea that I can change everything.

I recognize that others are involved in the equation. Because **God designed us to live and work with people, not puppets,** I accept that I will not always get my way.

As an adult, **I have the option of walking away from any situation that I deem to be unhealthy.** When I choose to remain in a situation, however, I am choosing to allow the others involved to voice and act upon their own opinions.

I can - and do - express myself on issues that matter to me or my community, but I let go of the idea that I can change other people against their will. ***My faith is in God not men,*** that includes myself.

Because I let go of the idea that I can somehow mold people or situations to my liking, I am free from the stress of feeling responsible for things outside of my control. I trust God with the things that are beyond my own ability.

Self-Reflection Questions:

1. Am I treating my family and peers as people or puppets?

2. Have I been trying to do God's job by attempting to change any situation that is outside my control?

3. Do I need to move on from a particular situation that I find unhealthy?

Day 16: Unnecessary

I choose not to allow unnecessary stress to control me.

*Therefore humble yourselves under the mighty hand of God, that He may exalt you in due time, **casting all your care upon Him**, for He cares for you.*
I Peter 5:7

I let go of unnecessary stress in my life to make way for the peace of Christ. I recognize the value of peace for my health, productivity and relationships.

I consciously embrace the peace of Christ when I find myself facing stressors and I refuse to waste energy on things that are outside my control.

While I recognize that there are situations in my life that will cause stress regardless of what I do, I assess each situation to determine if this stress is beneficial or pointless. I know I am free to remove that stressor from my life.

I can choose how stress affects me and how I respond to this glitch in my day. If I am stuck in a traffic jam, for example, I choose to see it as an opportunity to listen to audio books or sing along with my favorite songs.

Stress does not control me or dictate what kind of day I am having. *I surrender myself to the Holy Spirit within me – and allow myself to be led by the Spirit.* I choose to fix my mind on Christ and not on my problems, because this path leads to greater peace and productivity.

Self-Reflection Questions:

1. Are there any unnecessary stressors in my life that I can eliminate?

2. Why do I hang onto things that unnecessarily stress me out?

3. What is a common, but unavoidable, source of stress that I could respond to more positively, as empowered by the Holy Spirit?

Day 17: Stress Filter

Christ is my firewall that filters out stress.

For from him and through him and to him are all things. To him be the glory forever! Amen.
Romans 11:36

I can build a firewall that filters out stress and helps me reclaim my success when I view things through Christ.

I have let go of the idea that I need to be able to see my whole life at once. That's simply impossible. But I know God gave me my talents and interests for a purpose: so that I can *use* them to glorify Him!

By taking the time to discover my talents and pursue my interests, **I am working with my natural bent** rather than trying to force myself to be something I was never intended to be.

I invest in seeking God's will for my life. Because I am here for a purpose, it only makes sense that I do whatever I need to do to fulfill that purpose. Undoubtedly that costs time, energy, and money, and I am open to that.

When I know God's will for my life, I pursue it wholeheartedly. I enjoy the journey that He has set before me. **I am open and flexible to exploring** *different avenues as my love for Christ grows and develops.*

I resist the tendency to want to become a slave to myself. Instead, Christ is my compass, I remain eager to fully explore and experience each step of my journey with Him.

Self-Reflection Questions:

1. Am I allowing myself to be what I was created to be?

2. Do I have goals that I use to focus my plans and activities?

3. Do I serve my goals or do they serve me?

Day 18: Stress Outlet

Spending time with God is my outlet to relieve the stress in my life.

Answer me when I call to you, O my righteous God. Give me relief from my distress; be merciful to me and hear my prayer.

Psalm 4:1

Spending time with God is my outlet to relieve the stress in my life and engaging in it regularly is a priority for me. I know I am happiest and most productive when I have regular time with God, so I view these times as equally important as my work.

It is my choice in how I spend my time relieving stress. I may choose to pray, read, worship, go out for a run, or have a relaxing bubble bath. There is no one right way to spend time with God.

God knows my mind and body better than anyone, so I engage in activities that satisfy and nurture my relationship with Him.

Even though I work, take care of my family, and do everything that is part of being a productive, adult member of society, I plan time for myself and God regularly.

I maintain balance in my life. I recognize that work is good; however, I avoid the tendency to take this to an extreme and become a slave to my job!

I give my time with God as much priority as I do my work projects. I know I can be my best self only if I take the time and opportunity meet with Him regularly.

Self-Reflection Questions:

1. When do I communicate with God the best?

2. Do I give my time with God as much priority as my work?

3. Do I make my own decisions regarding how I spend time my time with God?

Day 19: Conflict Resolution

I can resolve personal conflicts peacefully.

But the fruit of the Spirit is love, joy, peace, longsuffering, kindness, goodness, faithfulness, gentleness, self-control. Against such there is no law.
Galatians 5:22-23

When trouble comes my way I can peacefully resolve the issue.

God has given me love and I use it to help resolve any conflicts that arise in my life. Resolving conflicts quickly with a peaceful nature is a way that I can bring glory to God.

I let go of fear, frustration and resentment. I embrace kindness, gentleness, goodness, and self-control in conflict resolution because it is what is right.

I am able to love others in tense situations and I look at the conflict from both sides. It pleases God when I view my conflicts in a Christ-like way and deal with them peacefully.

The Holy Spirit and the fruit it is developing in my life helps me to face my conflicts with confidence. **I am a peace-maker.**

Today I will let go of negative emotions and face conflicts fearlessly. I will embrace the fruit of the Spirit and solve my problems in a peaceful manner. I will resolve my conflicts and enjoy the serenity that comes from glorifying God.

Self-Reflection Questions:

1. Do I have any personal conflicts in my life right now that I can resolve peacefully?

2. How does the fruit of the Spirit affect the way I handle conflicts?

3. Have I let go of fear and resentments?

Day 20: Relaxation

I actively seek out relaxation in my life.

The LORD is my Shepherd; I shall not want. He makes me to lie down in green pastures; He leads me beside the still waters. He restores my soul; He leads me in the paths of righteousness for His name's sake.
Psalm 23: 1-3

I allow Christ, my Shepherd, to create an atmosphere of relaxation within my life.

Instead of waiting for a time to sit back and relax, I proactively make this time for myself. I am aware of my schedule and I make time for Christ in my life and special activities that I find relaxing. By scheduling time to be with Jesus and do the things that recharge my spirit, I become a more centered person.

I pay attention to how busy I allow myself to get and I ensure time is allotted to spend with Christ and do the things I enjoy doing. ***I allow myself to rearrange my schedule to make spending quality time with Jesus a high priority.*** Whether it is taking a peaceful stroll through the park, or spending time writing out my thoughts and prayers, I make time for a date with Jesus.

My time and my schedule are important, however, my serenity and relaxation is equally important to me. This is why I purposefully make time to step away from my busy life and simply breathe in calmness in Christ's presence.

Today I choose to create the time I need to seek Christ and the relaxation and peace He brings. I may simply need a half hour to feel recharged and **today I will schedule this time for myself.**

Self-Reflection Questions:

1. When managing my time have I allotted time for Jesus?

2. What activities do I find relaxing?

3. How will I devote 20 minutes a day to relaxing in Christ's presence?

4. When will I schedule an hour long "date" with just Jesus?

Day 21: Moving Forward

I release my sins to God; I have no use for them.

I acknowledged my sin to You, and my iniquity I have not hidden. I said, "I will confess my transgressions to the LORD," And You forgave the iniquity of my sin.
Psalm 32:5

I can finally let go of the things that have impeded me from moving forward, because I know that I have been forgiven.

God has given me direction in life and goals He desires me to achieve. I will reach the destinations and goals He has planned for me with His help.

All my past sins are behind me; I have let go of them, knowing that God has done the same. I am free now to move into the positive directions that He has set out for me. **Through faith in Christ I forge on, moving forward without fear.**

I have let go of all of the things that were holding me back in life, knowing that with God all things are possible. I am living a positive life, free from the bondage of sin.

I let go of the sinful need to please anyone but Christ and this frees me. I let go of the need to put too many expectations on myself because I know this doesn't glorify God and is putting my trust in myself instead of Him.

With God's help I can achieve my goals in the time that I am supposed to; I let go of timelines that hold me back, accepting that God's timing is better than my own.

I let go of the sin of pushing myself until I am exhausted; this does not display trust in Christ. I give myself the rest and time I need to have more energy to be a productive person, knowing that God grants sleep to those He loves.

Today, I let go of the sins in my life that are holding me back. I replace them with an overabundance of love, joy, faith, and trust in Christ.

I can move at God's pace and let go of an unrealistic timetable. I will be the person God created me to be at all times and let go of being different to different people. ***Today I live without fear of, or bondage to, sin.***

Self-Reflection Questions:

1. Do I feel free to pursue the goals God gave me?

2. Have I let go of the things that hold me back?

3. Have I looked at what may be making me feel under pressure?

Day 22: Constructive Communication

I communicate positively and peacefully.

Let no corrupt word proceed out of your mouth, but what is good for necessary edification, that it may impart grace to the hearers.
Ephesians 4:29

I exchange words and feelings with others in a positive and calm manner.

When I communicate with others, I first make sure that I am in a positive frame of mind. I do my best to be aware of the things I wish to convey to them. I gracefully speak words of constructive criticism, refraining from speaking words meant to tear others down.

I remove myself from feelings of anger and frustration before I engage in communications. Preparing myself in this way allows me to remain calm and communicate constructively as God instructs me to.

It is difficult to communicate with others when they feel defensive. I am able to lower their defenses and provide a peaceful stage for constructive communication. This opens the door for others to communicate in a positive way as well.

I feel strong, and in control because of who God made me not because I assert myself over others. **My constructive way of communicating encourages those around me,** instead of tearing them down. I know I am fair in my dealings with others.

Today I choose to communicate in a calm, constructive way that offers a peaceful environment. I remain positive no matter what happens and feel confident in the fact that I can walk away if I need to.

I feel good about my ability to remain positive and peaceful in my communications with the help of my Savior.

Self-Reflection Questions:

1. How can I calm myself before communicating?

2. Have I taken the time to understand the situation at hand?

3. Have I communicated my thoughts and feelings constructively?

Day 23: Medicating Stress

I medicate my stress symptoms with shots of joy and praise.

And my soul shall be joyful in the LORD; it shall rejoice in His salvation.
                                                        Psalm 35:9

There are many ways I cope with stress. Although relaxation and prayer are strong against stress, **my favorite anti-stress agent is joy.** I love to rejoice in the Lord! I allow myself to rejoice and praise God even in the midst of anxiety.

God created life to be enjoyed. I praise God for my life and live a life of joy. The joy of the Lord is my strength.

Rejoicing in my salvation can change my outlook and help me cope with stressful times. Praising God helps me when I can't see past my situation.

Instead of allowing stress to damage my spirit, **I use joy to turn stress into fuel.** When I remember that God is perfecting me in the midst of a stressful time, I can press on with new resolve. Taking time to rejoice and praise God during a stressful situation helps me relax and regain focus.

When I rejoice during stressful times, I send myself a message of acceptance. I tell myself that it is okay to be human because God is in control. I can be a witness to those around me by living out my faith and trust in Christ.

When I praise God during stressful moments, I remind myself that God is always good, and He uses all things together for the good of those who love Him and are called according to His purpose.

Whether it is a quick smile caused by remembering God's provision or a prayer of thanks and praise, joy is my medicine of choice.

Self-Reflection Questions:

1. When was the last time I put my responsibilities on hold and praised God for His sovereignty?

2. How can I use joy to relieve my stress?

3. What are the things that make me rejoice?

Day 24: Talk it Out

I am able to combat stress by talking things out with Christ and others.

My soul, wait silently for God alone, for my expectation is from Him. He only is my rock and my salvation; He is my defense; I shall not be moved...Trust in Him at all times, you people; **Pour out your heart before Him**; *God is a refuge for us.*
Psalm 62:5-8

When a situation is causing me stress, I speak up and **<u>pour out my heart</u> to Christ** through prayer instead of letting things get bottled up inside of me. I am not afraid to share my inmost thoughts with Jesus. He will not judge me and is the only person I can fully trust with my secret thoughts and feelings.

Sometimes, Christ may lead me to share my thoughts with others. **When appropriate, talking things out with others opens avenues for better communication.**

In my relationships, I have the right to be heard. I have the right to express my point of view and for others to listen because I have valid things to say. However, those rights also carry the responsibility to be respectful in my speech.

If someone is doing something that upsets me, I can speak to them respectfully without losing my temper. Christ's Spirit in me gives me control of my emotions. My emotions are not in control of me. I choose to use my words carefully in stressful situations and allow Christ to lead me in what I say.

Often, I find that I am stressed because I misunderstood something that was said. **Open lines of communication help to minimize confusion.** I work better when I feel like I am understood by others.

I stay away from violence because it solves nothing. Violence only leads me to feel more stressed than before. It leaves me feeling embarrassed and defeated. **When I want to be understood, gentle words are my main form of defense.**

A soft answer turns away wrath, but a harsh word stirs up anger.
Proverbs 15:1

I have sharp communication skills because I am led by the Holy Spirit. I allow Christ's Spirit in me to give me the words to say when I am involved in a dispute. My vocabulary is sprinkled with kindness. When I speak with gentleness, others are more than willing to reach an agreement with me.

Self-Reflection Questions:

1. What has stopped me from talking things out _with Christ_ through prayer? What has stopped me from talking things out with _others_ in the past?

2. How can I allow Christ to control me and my responses instead of my emotions?

3. The next time I feel like lashing out in anger, how can I change my response to one of gentleness and kindness instead?

Day 25: Balancing Life

I am melting the extra pounds of negative stress away by balancing my intake of duties, expectations, and pressures.

Therefore we also, since we are surrounded by so great a cloud of witnesses, let us lay aside every weight, and the sin which so easily ensnares us, and let us run with endurance the race that is set before us, looking unto Jesus, the author and finisher of our faith, who for the joy that was set before Him endured the cross, despising the shame, and has sat down at the right hand of the throne of God.
                                                Hebrews 12:1-2

My life is in balance. By prayerfully prioritizing, I create my own pyramid of responsibilities. My priorities are my guidelines for how I spend my time, energy and money.

In order to stay balanced, I do not over indulge in any one area. With God's help **I set limits for myself so that I can stay healthy.** Balancing my responsibilities is my exercise. When I stay the course, I burn off the excess weight of busywork or distractions. My life is more fulfilling when I replace busywork with meaningful tasks that bring glory to God.

I remove anxiety from my diet and replace it with prayerful planning. I balance my duties by filling out my planner. If I see that I have too many tasks on one day, I stop adding responsibilities for that date or move something to another day if necessary.

Sometimes I have to say "no" to things or people. Other times I simply have to say "not now." If I tried to do it all and neglected to limit my activities, I would burn myself out and experience negative stress. I acknowledge my God given limits.

My expectations are fair. If others place unrealistic expectations on me, I ask God for guidance, and then humbly suggest more realistic goals if necessary. *I take on reasonable challenges.* I am encouraged when I exceed my expectations. If I set my expectations too high and then I miss, I would be stressed and discouraged.

When I feel myself getting buried under pressure, I know it's time to re-evaluate my diet. *It does not glorify God when I overload myself.* There is a difference between taking on a challenge and simply taking on too much.

When I melt away negative stress I fit into the clothes of joy and peace of mind that God has made for me.

Self-Reflection Questions:

1. How do I prepare for the tasks and projects in my life?

2. How do prayer and preparation ease my stress and strain?

3. How could I take a more proactive approach to reach my goals?

Day 26: Achieving Peace

I am constantly achieving peace in my life through prayer.

Finally, brethren, whatever things are true, whatever things are noble, whatever things are just, whatever things are pure, whatever things are lovely, whatever things are of good report, if there is any virtue and if there is anything praiseworthy—meditate on these things.
                                                    Philippians 4:8

I make it a point to foster peace in my life, because I put my trust in God.

I slow down to allow God's peace into my mind. If a harsh thought attempts to assault me when I start to relax, I commit it to God. I choose to be still, knowing that there are far more peaceful, positive thoughts to protect me against mental assault.

I train and reward my mind by actively following thoughts that are true, noble, just, pure and lovely while allowing the negative ones to fall away unattended. **Negative thoughts, left unfed, will die off.** They do not distress me by their presence, because I trust God and I allow them to come and go without any direct attention from me.

Prayer is the gateway to peace, through which I find health, wholeness, and productivity. By taking time to settle down and open myself up to God, I achieve a richer and more fulfilling life.

Self-Reflection Questions:

1. In what ways do I foster God's peace in my life?

2. Do I allow my fear of negative thoughts to keep my mind too busy for my own good? Why?

3. In what way can I open myself up to God's peace today?

Day 27: Praise & Worship

Praise and worship rejuvenate my soul.

I will praise You, O LORD, with my whole heart; I will tell of all Your marvelous works. I will be glad and rejoice in You; I will sing praise to Your name, O Most High.
Psalm 9:1-2

I take time to retreat from the noise of life and find a quiet place where I can praise my God. Daily, I make it a point to turn off distractions and focus on what is going on inside my heart and mind. When I reflect upon what God has done in my life, I can't help but worship Him.

I praise God through my actions and words. My countenance reveals that which is hidden deep inside of me. **When I am thankful within my soul, I am able to accomplish more than I ever imagined.**

I live every day of my life with a heart full of worship; free from stress because I trust in God my Savior. The small annoyances of daily life are incapable of stealing my joy because I focus on the bigger picture. When I take things lightly and guard myself from worry by giving my cares to God, I preserve my health. My heart and soul are healthy when I let go of the things out of my control quickly and only hold onto the things that God has in trusted to me.

Worship refreshes my soul like the streams of a fountain washing away all anxiety and fear. I am bold and confident in my future when I praise my Creator and listen to His voice.

There comes a point where I must stop trying to make sense of everything and simply rely on faith. Praise and worship rescue me from the pit of the mundane and becoming complacent.

Today, I choose to drown out the noise all around me and focus on the voice calling my name. I am turning away from distractions and taking time to praise Jesus Christ my Savior.

Self-Reflection Questions:

1. Am I tuning in to the right voice?

2. How can I turnoff the noise around me and praise my God?

3. What are my actions saying about the state of my inner being?

Day 28: Stressful Situations

I like the way I handle stressful situations.

The LORD is my strength and my shield; My heart trusted in Him, and I am helped; Therefore my heart greatly rejoices, And with my song I will praise Him.
Psalm 28:7

I do not fear stressful situations because I know I handle them in a healthy and productive way. I feel good about the way I handle stressful situations because my trust is in the Lord.

I trust that I can rise to the top when there is a situation that is difficult to handle with God's help. I am able to remain calm and assess the problem at hand quickly and effectively because He is at work within me. He helps me understand what is going on and what needs to happen in order to resolve the problem quickly. **He has given me a skilled and steady hand that can overcome any tense dilemma.**

Taking charge of challenging situations and delegating responsibilities to others is what God has prepared me to do. **My trust in God is how I am able to handle stressful situations with ease.**

Today I will take on any challenges that arise and I do so with patience, diligence, and trust. I know I can handle challenging circumstances with God's help and I will take necessary measures to smooth out difficulties as He would have me do.

Self-Reflection Questions:

1. Do I trust God to help me through challenging situations?

2. Who will I delegate responsibilities to during times of stress?

3. How am I able to use my God given strengths?

Day 29: No Pressure

I can live a pressure-free, healthy life with focus, clarity, direction, and purpose.

For this is the love of God, that we keep His commandments. And His commandments are not burdensome. For whatever is born of God overcomes the world. And this is the victory that has overcome the world—our faith.
1 John 5:3-4

I use my tools of prayer, faith, trust and worship to remain healthy and light-hearted.

I am able to freely move through my day with peace of mind and a joyful heart. I feel this serenity because I have fortified myself with healthy spiritual habits. I trust God with every area in my life and thus I can feel pressure-free. **I am centered and grounded because I remain on focused Christ each and every moment of my day.**

I am fully aware of where I am going and where I wish to be, which brings me closer toward my goals every day. **My day and my life are full of purposeful thought, prayer and action.** Blending this in my life offers me serenity and peace.

When difficulty or pressure comes into my life, I am able to handle it with speed and ease using the tools and skills God has given me in the Scriptures. I keep my body healthy with nutritious foods and invigorating

exercise, which opens my eyes to a new level of conscious living.

My mind is clear and I am able to be attentive. God has given me an understanding of my goals and how to achieve them. This makes me strong and able to overcome any uncomfortable situation or pressure that may come my way with the help of my Savior.

Today I choose to remain confident in God's ability to help me overcome adversity and live a pressure-free life by trusting in Him. *I will use the tools God has given me to handle anything that may come my way.* I have built healthy habits that strengthen and prepare me for my life-long journey.

Self-Reflection Questions:

1. What tools do I have at my disposal?

2. How have I fortified my body and mind?

3. What keeps me centered and focused on Christ?

Day 30: Pursuing Christ

My life is full of peace and happiness.

Therefore let us pursue the things which make for peace and the things by which one may edify another.
Romans 14:19

My life is full of peace and happiness because ***I am pursuing a personal relationship with Christ.*** I am confident that I am on the right path because I use and develop the interests and talents that my Creator has instilled in me to glorify Him.

I have let go of the notion that I should be something I was not created to be. When I focus on developing my spiritual gifts and glorifying God, I achieve peace and a sense of harmony.

I am productive because I am working within the perimeters God has given me.

I look forward to fellowship with other Christians, we encourage one another. I glean strategies for success and decide whether or not they would suit my walk with God. But I reject the idea that anyone else's path is more important than my own.

A healthy family, community, or society has a variety of different roles and functions, each one vital to the well-being of the whole. Some are more visible than others and some tend to garner more applause, but all are equally important.

I let go of the temptation to do things just to receive the applause of others. Instead, **I focus on developing my true beauty in Christ,** knowing that this is what makes me most productive and brings me true peace and happiness.

Self-Reflection Questions:

1. Am I trying to adopt someone else's purpose in life?

2. Whose approval am I seeking by my actions?

3. What am I doing to fulfill *God's* purpose in my life?

Conclusion:

I Have Overcome Anxiety and Stress Through Christ's Transforming Power and I Know:

1. I can handle all stress by trusting God.

2. Stressful moments do not blind me from what is true.

3. Fear cannot penetrate my inner being.

4. A little prayer and preparation takes me a long way in easing strain and stress.

5. I refuse to worry when priorities change.

6. Prayerful planning allows me to complete my tasks without stress.

7. Faith in Christ enables me to find peace of mind.

8. Prayer is my rock during stressful moments.

9. I trust God with the things I cannot control.

10. I wholly accept difficulties in my life. God is using my trials to perfect me.

11. I do not sweat the small stuff.

12. I give my problems to God and have no reason to harbor tension.

13. I will remain calm through prayer and trust in God.

14. Because I am organized, I am able to minimize daily stress.
15. I can manage stress because I know I cannot control everything.

16. I choose not to allow unnecessary stress to control me.
17. Christ is my firewall that filters out stress.

18. Spending time with God is my outlet to relieve the stress in my life.

19. I can resolve personal conflicts peacefully.

20. I actively seek out relaxation in my life.

21. I release my sins to God; I have no use for them.

22. I communicate positively and peacefully.

23. I medicate my stress symptoms with shots of joy and praise.

24. I am able to combat stress by talking things out with Christ and others.

25. I am melting the extra pounds of stress away by balancing my intake of duties, expectations, and pressures.

26. I am constantly achieving peace in my life through prayer.

27. Praise and worship rejuvenate my soul.

28. I like the way I handle stressful situations.

29. I can live a pressure-free, healthy life with focus, clarity, direction, and purpose.

30. My life is full of peace and happiness.

Bonus: 20 MP3's

We have a bonus gift for you as a purchaser of the Kindle version of this eBook. It is 20 MP3's containing affirmations and scriptures on the following topics:

- Faith
- Forgiveness
- God
- Hope
- Jesus
- Love
- Mercy
- Prayer
- The Beatitudes
- The Message

Download your 20 bonus MP3's by visiting the following link: www.bodyandsoulpublishing.com/20mp3

We pray God impacts your life through His Word!

About The Author

Shelley Hitz

Shelley Hitz has been writing and publishing books since 2008. She is also the author of the website, FindYourTrueBeauty.com that reaches thousands of girls each month around the world. Her openness and vulnerability as she shares her own story of hope and healing will inspire and encourage you.

Shelley has been ministering to teens since 1998 alongside her husband, CJ. They currently travel and speak to teens and adults around the country. Shelley's main passion is to share God's truth and the freedom in Christ she has found with others. She does this through her books, websites and speaking engagements. You can find more about Shelley at her website: www.BodyandSoulPublishing.com

Read CJ and Shelley's Best-Selling Books:

21 Days of Gratitude Challenge
by Shelley Hitz

Unshackled and Free: True Stories of Forgiveness
by CJ and Shelley Hitz

The Forgiveness Formula: Finding Lasting Freedom in Christ
by CJ and Shelley Hitz

Fuel for the Soul: 21 Devotionals that Nourish
by CJ Hitz

Mirror Mirror…Am I Beautiful? Looking Deeper to Find Your True Beauty
by Shelley Hitz

Teen Devotionals…for Girls!
By Shelley Hitz and Heather Hart

Love Getting Free Christian Books?

Get notified of our book promotions
and download Shelley's ebook,
"How to Find Free Christian Books Online" at:

www.bodyandsoulpublishing.com/freebooks

www.ingramcontent.com/pod-product-compliance
Lightning Source LLC
Chambersburg PA
CBHW060350050426
42449CB00011B/2917